THE WORLD ACCORDING TO TERESA DI SCLAFANI

TERESA DI SCLAFANI DE NASCA

TecnoTur
Publishing

Is there a book inside you?

CONTENTS

THE WORLD ACCORDING TO TERESA DI SCLAFANI

Published by TecnoTur Publishing

Editing: TecnoTur Publishing team

Internal layout: Allan Tépper

Covers, spine and back cover: Andreína Ascanio Toro

ISBN of the paperback:

979-8-9890652-9-5

ISBN of the electronic version (ebook):

979-8-9905171-0-3

ISBN of the audiobook:

979-8-9905171-1-0

DEDICATION

In honor of my husband who died 15 years ago, October 8, 2008,
my children and grandchildren.

CHAPTER 1

CAPITALS OF THE WORLD

- Italy: capital Rome
- Russia: capital Moscow
- Germany: capital Berlin
- France: capital Paris
- England: capital London
- United States: capital Washington, DC
- Puerto Rico: capital San Juan
- Colombia: capital Bogotá
- Ecuador: capital Quito
- Dominican Republic: capital Santo Domingo
- Perú: capital Lima
- Bolivia: capital La Paz
- Venezuela: capital Caracas
- Haiti: capital Port-au-Prince
- Ukraine: capital Kiev
- Nicaragua: capital Managua

- Chile: capital Santiago
- Paraguay: capital Asunción
- Honduras: capital Tegucigalpa
- China: economic capital Shanghai

CHAPTER 2
WORLD HISTORY AND MONARCHY

- Philip, King of Belgium and Germany, married Matilda, a native of Warsaw from an aristocratic family.
- King Balbino, grandson of King Manuel III, married Paola 2002.
- King Balbino's son, a prince, wanted to go to Rome but could not enter because he was in an asylum. Pope John Paul II interceded so that he could go to Rome. He became involved in politics with success. He devoted himself to dancing, singing, sports and won a competition with a song he dedicated to Italy.
- King Emmanuel Albert III of Savoy.
- Princess Victoria, daughter of the King of Sweden.
- Charles Gustav VI, the military son, married Schel. He was a wealthy man, had an estate and a mine. He married in Mecca.

- Emperor Di Sclafani was born in Germany and was the son of Giovanni, Count Di Sclafani. He went to fight helping Emperor Charlemagne in Lombardy. He then went to Palermo and built the Royal Monastery of the Trinitarians (which today is the Military Hospital Las Trinitarias), the Church of Providence, the Church of St. Augustine and the Church of Nicolo Dell'arcadia. In 1330 the Count went to Sicily in the service of William the Bad.
- Simón Bolívar united Gran Colombia (aka Greater Colombia) in 1819.
- Independence of Bolivia 1825.
- Independence of Venezuela 1811.
- Independence of the United States 1776.
- Cristoforo Colombo, known in Castilian as Cristóbal Colón and in English as Christopher Columbus, discovered America in 1492.
- King of England, Philip Edward.
- Queen Elizabeth.
- In 1945 the United States dropped an atomic bomb, 2,000,000 people died.
- Dictator Franco of Spain sent King Felipe de Borbón into exile in Rome.
- King Juan Carlos de Borbón was born in Rome.
- Germany waged a border war between México and the United States over a sinking ship.
- In 1989 they negotiated diplomatically with Russian President Gorbachev and the Soviet Union was later eliminated.

- 1939 Japan attacked the United States to prevent its military plans that year.
- Napoleon Bonaparte, known as a French military leader, became famous during the French Revolution. He became the de facto leader of the French Republic. He was the first consul from 1799 to 1804.
- Fidel Castro Dictator of Cuba 1960
- Jimmy Carter in 1976 went to Cuba. He was a true socialist.
- Giuseppe Garibaldi, Italian, was a successful general and revolutionary patriot. He contributed to the Italian unification. He slept one night in the village of Alia.
- Act of Union, Anglo-Irish Treaty. May 1, 1707 - January 1, 1801 - April 12, 1922.
- Argentina, dictator Juan Domingo Perón. His wife was Isabel Perón.
- 1917 Mexican Revolution, where men and women fought.
- Somoza Dictator.
- In 1998 Pope John Paul II visited Cuba.
- In Chile in 1973, the dictator was Salvador Allende.
- Jorge Rafael Videla, dictator of Argentina from 1976 to 1981.
- Marcello Levin Alejandro Agustil Lamine 1971 and 1973.

- 1942 Poland was an enemy of the European Union for being against Russia and in agreement with Ukraine.
- Germany 10th century, Otto the Great intervened in Italy.
- 11th century Conrad.
- Twelfth century in northern Italy, Frederick Barbarossa confronted the Pope,
- Frederick XII ruled by Prince,
- Rudolph XIII made a reform to protect Naples.
- Sixteenth century questioned English practice, reformed by Martin Luther.
- Emperor Charles V the Catholic. With the war of 1555 it was divided from Christianity and the war lasted 30 years.
- Eighteenth century economy destroyed Brandenburg, Russia, with landowner support of mercantilism.
- XVIII century, Frederick, King of Russia, militarized the city and Austria, keeping part of the territory.
- XIX century, Napoleon Bonaparte could not stay for long. They didn't leave and he got sick because of the cold.
- A lot of liberalism and nationalism.
- Frederick William IV created a new constitution.
- XVI century, Russia formed a customs house and railroad, eliminating compulsory military service. Russia wanted to save money and do important things.

- 1862 Otto von Bismarck.
- 1864-66 Austrian.
- 1870-71- Wilhelm I, Second German Empire.
- France opened several banks.
- Charlemagne, first emperor of Rome. The empire was divided.
- Philip 1, 1060-1192.
- 1214 Frederick, the emperor. It lasted until March 15, 1217. Many bad situations occurred, the land was not productive. Then they gave the land to the peasants and entrepreneurs to make the land productive, resulting in large exports of various items. It was in agreement with the whole world. It extracted coal and minerals.
- The reservists rose up, who were peasants themselves. They took criminals out of the jails and looted businesses and houses.
- In 1807 and 1809, the military killed 9,000 people.
- If the monarchy had lasted until 1950, everyone would have lived very well.
- In the European Union in 1907, the democrats were very strong. The peasants were happy, because they wanted a union. The center-right democracy and communism were formed.
- 1917 Lenin, dictator, fought for revolutions. Then Stalin appointed a provisional government in 4 weeks.
- 3 years of civil war with Lenin.

- Marines and military wanted to overthrow the government. 50,000 soldiers set up a provisional government.
- Niboleschi, revolutionary socialist.
- They denounced the army on January 5, 1918 for treason. The democrats launched a civil war between communists and democrats. They enacted compulsory military service in 1922 and 25. The volunteer army turned against Russia and went to Czechoslovakia.
- 1919 and -20, Russia invaded Poland.
- In 1921 there was hatred, hunger and misery.
- In 1961 came Gorbachev.
- 77 years since Russia defeated Nazi Germany.
- On May 9, 1945, the war in Europe ended.

CHAPTER 3
EVITA PERÓN

Evita Perón, deceased for more than 70 years, was the wife of Juan Domingo Perón (the president of Argentina during the 20th century). She died at the age of 33 of cervical cancer.

Evita's corpse was embalmed and lost, but they found it after 16 years. It was first retrieved in Italy and then in Spain. The corpse was hidden and given to Perón. That is what the legend says, that it was a body without a grave. They negotiated to return the corpse to Perón with the de facto government of Pedro Eugenio Aramburu.

Evita was the most relevant figure in Argentina and was a much loved character.

CHAPTER 4
HISTORY OF FREEMASONRY

A secret school of learning, whose motto is «liberty, equality and fraternity». Their teachings are always consistent. and the word Mason means bricklayer. They used geometry as insignia, the triangle system and its identifications.

No one can know the secret of Freemasonry. No one reveals the secrets, neither drunk, nor drugged, nor sick, and it is a secret that is taken to the grave. The ruler, the compass and the eye is the insignia of the Masons. To enter the brotherhood the person has to be investigated. If they make a mistake and the person who enters is not good, they are kept without a degree and are never given one.

There are 6,000,000 Masons in the world. The Masons could not control the world and outside the temple they are normal, hard-working people. It is not a sect and they can have any religion. A Mason cannot be an atheist; he has to believe in God. Every Mason is recognized by the salute and the three dots on the signatures.

On St. John's Day, June 24, a symbolic baptism is held and they are given a medal with a Masonic insignia. When someone is initiated into Freemasonry, they are given a white apron called a pennant, which they have to wear when they die. They can also wear a ring and medal with Masonic insignia, if it is not a 33rd degree.

Before, no one knew where the lodges were, since the place was secret. Then the lodges were apparent to the whole world. The lodges are all the same: the ceiling, the black and white floor, and the paintings are all the same. There is an Honorable and a Secretary and all the temples in all countries have had the freedom for all to attend.

The Freemasons made history by revolting against the Church. Sixteen thousand Masons and Jews were killed. Seeing that they formed a red triangle, built the subway airport in Colorado and tried to change the world. Freemasonry has 21 hospitals in the United States, one in México and one in Canada, called Shriners Hospital for Children.

They wrote a lot and many famous people were thought to be Masons, such as Simon Bolivar. In Argentina, the dictator wanted to know Masonic secrets. President Alfonsín was a Mason and was not well regarded by the military.

The Grand Lodge suffered one of the greatest repressions in Germany, where 4000 people were seized in the year 1442. They were excommunicated in 1768, -83 and -97 for not agreeing with what the Church was doing. Pope V reversed their excommunications.

CHAPTER 5

CHARLEMAGNE

Charlemagne was King of the Franks and a Roman Emperor. In his infancy he was baptized by Pope Stephen III and when he was 6 years old he promised the Pope that everyone would be baptized.

In 752, the King of the Franks preached «freedom or death». In his youth Charlemagne inherited some mansions in Paris, eight swords and a shield, weapons of warriors. At the age of 15 he was given the swords because he had to fight with the Saxons against the pagans. At that time the Roman Empire was ruled by Emperor Constantine, in 754.

Charlemagne cursed the pagans who had betrayed their King and waged a dirty war. In the year 782, 4500 men died in battle. Charlemagne, King of the Franks, and all his followers, who spent many years of war and never surrendered, are remembered in that period. «Freedom or death», they shouted.

In the war with the Saxons, they converted them to

Christianity, always maintaining piety for the enemies and with those who became Christians. Charlemagne escaped to Rome, made a castle for the government and built cathedrals with highest domes of all temples.

In the year 800 he was given the title of Emperor and was crowned on Christmas Day by Pope Leo III, who crowned an Emperor for the first time. Before Charlemagne, the Emperor was always Roman and for the first time an Emperor of French origin was crowned. When he became Emperor of Rome, he was crowned with a crown of gold and diamonds.

Although he could neither read nor write, Charlemagne made many educational reforms including the teaching of writing. He promoted monasteries, churches and Bible study during his Empire. In his quest for learning, he came into contact with the cultures of Spain and England. Among other things, Charlemagne decreed Sundays off. In the year 875 they were still satisfied with Charlemagne.

CHAPTER 6

BRIEF ROMAN HISTORY

- 500 years before Christ, Emperor Julius Caesar Italy.
- Year 43, there was a battle won by the Romans.
- Year 260, the emperor built a wall 180 kilometers long.
- Year 455 the Romans were divided.
- Year 601, the battle of Antonio Reyes Conkin.
- Year 670, Constantine IV wasEmperor and fought against invaders.
- Year 703, John Albert was baptized as a Catholic.
- Pichincha.
- Year 879, Alfred the Great was crowned.
- Year 1015, under Danish control.
- Year 1066, King William I built St. Peter's Chapel.
- Years1016 and 1066, King William I ruled.
- Year1214 King Philip Augustus drafted the Magna Carta and introduced taxes.

- Year 1258, bankruptcy of England, because the statutes were not respected.
- Year 1260, Second Barons' War.
- The 100-year war.
- Year 1420, Henry V of England encountered French troops in Lombardy and won the victory.
- Henry V married Margherita and later died at the age of 35.
- Year 1435, Henry VI was of age.
- Year 1814, Charles VII died was buried in Rome.
- Germany begins a new history for the Germans, the Germanic Roman Empire.
- Charlemagne's peak was called the Third story.

CHAPTER 7
SAXON DYNASTY

- King Henry I lived in the castle of the Saxons.
- Year 933, King Otto I was crowned.
- Years 1036-1046, Henry III.
- Years 1056-1105, Conrad IV, 50 years.
- Year 1125, Henry V.
- Year 1137, the religious could not marry, they were concubines.
- Years 1138-1168, Frederick I, Barbarossa.
- Year 1198, Frederick II was born, reigned in Sicily from 1220 to 1250 and founded the University of Naples.
- Years 1268-1273, Salerno.

CHAPTER 8
WORLD WARS

WORLD WAR I

In 1917 U.S. troops arrived in Europe and began fighting the Germans. When the U.S. Marines (founded in 1817) entered battle, the Germans ordered a retreat and one of them said that «U.S. Marines were like fighting devils».

In 1918, the Germans launched an offensive to win the war with120 tanks. More than 1200 Germans were taken prisoner. The U.S. soldiers were very well prepared and the Germans surrendered. Therefore, the armistice was signed on November 11, 1918 at 10 am. The First World War left Europe devastated: 4 empires disappeared, 60 million soldiers died and 4 million mutilated.

On June 28, 1919, the Treaty of Versailles was signed, which established that the Germans will be responsible for the expenses caused by the war.

Between 1932 and 1933, after the First World War, the

extermination of the Ukrainians, also called Holomodor, took place. During these years a great famine occurred, possibly caused by Stalin, who claimed to create a new way of life. Ukrainians did not eat, they were with their bones outside. There was a call for death and children were dressed in military garb. The left was united with Stalin and the Nazis. Germany and Russia were allies with intent to conquer all of Europe. They murdered 20 million people.

THE BEGINNINGS OF ADOLF HITLER

Hitler had been wounded twice during World War I, in 1914 and 1918.

In August 1936 he inaugurated the Berlin Olympic Games as German Chancellor. Three weeks later he received the British minister, whose visit left him happy.

On June 18, 1937 a pilot accompanied them. By this time the communists had disappeared and there was no unemployment. During this year Hitler had a mistress for 4 years, named Eva Braun, whom he occasionally accompanied in an apartment. Her father was upset with the relationship, as they were a devout Catholic family. Eva had two suicide attempts, since she did not want to marry.

On September 28, 1938, Hitler was visited by Mussolini. That day they had a party and signed an agreement or alliance.

In March 1938, unification with Austria took place, something Hitler had always desired. Two weeks later, Czechoslovakia's fate was sealed. The following year he visited a small Austrian village where the children caled him «our hero».

WORLD WAR II

On September 1, 1939 Hitler invaded Poland, starting World War II. Two days later Italy and France declared war against Germany. Poland surrendered, including its weapons, amassing more than 70,000 deaths. As a nation, Poland ceased to exist when it was divided between Germany and the Soviet Union. Their plans included the elimination of Italy and France.

On May 10, 1940 the Battle of France began. Three thousand, five hundred and forty men abandoned France, leaving behind weapons and machine guns. British and French troops were defeated and left France across the English Channel. A German soldier wrote his wife that they had won in only four weeks, with the flag flying and the bells ringing.

Britain opposed surrender and said that the war would continue until one of the nations disappeared. Thus begins the Battle of Britain, aerial combat between the British and German air forces. Hitler said that he had excellent pilots and if the enemies dropped 4000 bombs, they would drop 200,000. More than 4,000 people died as a result of this fighting.

Hitler lost to England and began the extermination of the Jews. Hitler wanted Jews marked with a Star of David armband and chain. Every day 40 to 50 people died of starvation. The Nazis used the ancient religions in their conspiracies, and sent a group of priests by ship to India. Hitler had

Jewish blood, according to some theories, and he also had an astrologer.

Hitler abandoned his plans to invade England and decided to fight against Russia, because he wanted to eliminate communism and wage a war of extermination. For this purpose there were more than 3000 German soldiers against Russia and they all wanted victory. One of these soldiers wrote home saying that they planned to destroy Russia.

In 1941, Hitler and his generals failed to defeat Russia as Jews died. Hitler decided he wanted to defeat the Japanese. The German military wanted to withdraw, but Hitler objected. Two months later the Soviet army captured more than 1200 Germans, 90,000 Germans surrendered and 80,000 died in concentration camps. At the end of 1942, 1200 children and women were transferred.

On August 15, 1943, U.S. troops were stationed at Messina, Italy, having arrived on ships from Africa. After the attacks against the Germans and Italians, Messina was destroyed, but the Allies won. Once all the Germans had withdrawn and fascism had disappeared from the island of Sicily, the U.S.s created an atmosphere of normalcy.

Shortly after, the British army landed in Calabria to prepare for new combat. However, the landing fields were repaired by the Italian military, who were once again organized. Mechanics arrived to fix the airplanes and remains of German machinery. The British fought against the Italians and the Germans, risking the lives of many pilots when landing.

On September 8, 1943 Badoglio's soldiers landed at Salerno, for the war was not over. The Allies lost many men and the battle continued against the Italian navy ships. Finally, the Italian navy surrendered and declared that the war was over. Italy wanted to reclaim the settlements of all fleets, as the Italian navy was destroyed. In the end Italy gave up its entire navy, which was taken by Germany and Russia, and so the Italian navy embarked on a new era.

In Palermo everything was a party and the U.S. soldiers felt at home. They danced, sang, rode horses, played with the children, went to the square and bathed in the crystal clear water of Palermo. They brought tractor teams and cleaned all of Sicily. They went around all the villages with songs, throwing candies and chocolates to the children, who had never eaten them.

In 1944 the Normandy Landings took place. The U.S.s entered Europe with 8000 soldiers. The landing was difficult and affected them, with 60% of the soldiers having suffered from seasickness. Each soldier had a load of 45 kilos plus a heavy rifle. One thousand, four hundred and fifty soldiers died in the landing and a third of them died in the water. It was 6:42 in the morning and they were faring very badly. If they didn't get off the beach, they couldn't attack. The waves were two meters high. If the water was 80 centimeters, the rifle would fire and they would die. When the rifle fired at one meter, they were saved. When they got out there were thousands of dead.

The Germans, men trained for dangerous situations, thought they had failed. They recruited some peasants to fight. They sent out carrier pigeons and everywhere the Germans attacked. The English pushed on and reached the streets of Hamburg, which were burned to the ground.

During this same year, 1944, the French Allies left Britain to return to France. Even the children took up the fight. The Germans began to lose, abandoned by Hitler who was still leading the war. His health began to suffer and he manifested heart problems and Parkinson's disease.

For 12 years a team built a missile in secret. The Allies continued to advance and the Germans lost the war. On April 11, 1945, the Allies arrived at the concentration camp at Bambau, where a lone soldier survived. The crematorium was full. «If you survive, don't forget our fate.» The U.S. soldiers saw the disasters in the concentration camps.

On April 21, 1945 Soviet soldiers entered Berlin. About 28 million people were killed. Two million women, many German women were raped.

At this point Hitler did not know what to do and felt powerless. The war was over and he felt responsible for the failure. He married his mistress and wrote a speech or political testament to his followers. On April 30, 1945, Hitler committed suicide together with his now wife, Eva Braun.

In the last month the U.S. soldiers took over the streets of Tunis. They paraded in the streets in trucks. The Allies arrived in France, while the Italians were not happy. The U.S. military had left the Italians and after three years it was all over. The Italians had fought bravely.

CHAPTER 9
THE JEWS

The Jews had no homeland. Spain put them on a ship that was never received at any port. Nobody wanted them in their homeland until they arrived in Puerto Cabello, Venezuela. There they were welcomed with open arms; boys, girls and adults had a party.

In 1948 they were given a very small piece of land in Israel, where they made a garden. Today the Jewish community controls the world in wealth and through labor unions.

CHAPTER 10

THE MAFIA

SICILIAN MAFIA

The origins of the Mafia in Italy date back to 1812 in Sicily. Twenty thousand landowners were recruited to fill the vacuum of authority. Many countries had no police and, to control the bandits, Mafias were established, who were governed through the code of silence. Vito Cascio Ferro was a Mafia boss who commanded 8,000 men, stole cattle in quantity and killed people in Sicily and the Corleone district.

When Mussolini came to power, the Mafiosi were persecuted and a war in Palermo awaited them as the Fascists wanted to eliminate the Mafia. Several were killed and many moved with their families to the United States to traffic in drugs, cigarettes and alcohol.

A few years before World War II, the United States became the center of the Mafia, led by Al Capone. In order to consolidate their future, the Mafia had to establish itself in Latin America and the Mafia was organized in Cuba, so the Mafia celebrities spent New Year's there.

THE MAFIA IN CUBA

A young Lansky arrives in the United States in the 1920s, where he begins to pay and play cards. By 1928 Lansky became an advisor to Lucky Luciano, an Italian-U.S.-American, prominent in the mob world. Their business multiplied, so Lansky convinced Luciano to set up and launder money in Cuba and managed the business directly with the dictator Batista. Luciano is indicted and imprisoned, so the FBI said Luciano must move to the United States.

During World War II, Luciano was released from prison with the condition not to return to the United States and he went to Cuba, where he met with Batista. After several months Luciano became the head of the Latin American Mafia.

Cuba becomes a Mafia center and they start building hotels. Luciano's presence in Cuba was throwing the FBI off the scent and the Mafia told him not to go to Cuba anymore. Luciano abused the freedom of the island after being locked up. Luciano communicated with mobsters in the U.S. and told them he was entering on an Italian passport. He sent money deposits to Switzerland and also in Batista's name.

Meanwhile, Fidel Castro began to make his presence felt in Cuba. He is studying them and said he needs freedom, not revolutions. In 1952 Batista initiated a coup d'état and returned to power. Lansky turned Cuba into the best port, with many casinos that attracted US-Americans with their charm and comfort. Lansky revolutionized gambling.

Batista censured the casinos that did not comply with the laws, but the Mafia offered him guarantees so that the inhabitants would improve their standard of living. In the end it all went into the casinos' pockets. Lansky was concerned that Batista wanted a 50/50 split of profits, which did not suit them. Luciano and Lansky said that the Mafia was willing to negotiate with the revolutionary guerrillas, but only with the elimination of Batista.

In 1958 he waited for him at the Hotel Nacional and Batista said goodbye to the Mia. Lansky said that the new era began: «we have to start the new era, we have to take as much money as we can». In 1959 Fidel overthrew Batista and appointed himself commander, but he did not receive the mafia. Lansky fled with hundreds of thousands of dollars and went to *Miami*, although a Colombian had suggested he go to Medellin. By the time of his death at the age of 80, Lansky was the richest man in the United States.

On May 3, 1999, the Hotel Venezia opened in Las Vegas. It featured a 500-meter luxury shopping mall, first-class restaurant and canal with gondolas. One night cost U$425 for 2 adults and 2 children.

THE MAFIA IN MÉXICO

Virginia Hill, also known as the Mafia Queen, was one of the most important figures in organized crime. Virginia moved to Chicago to escape her violent husband and looked for a job in a bar. There she befriended a colonel, who helped her because she felt she was in danger. Thanks to her skills, she entered the Mafia and started to be part of the business.

Virginia joined Luciano in New York and the FBI moved to eliminate them, while Luciano made a fortune. Virginia traveled to Los Ángeles and started throwing big parties to make contacts.

She built the first casino in Las Vegas, the Flamingo Hotel, together with her lover Bugsy Siegel, another of Luciano's partners. The mob accused Virginia of transferring the money destined for the hotel to her personal accounts in Switzerland. She fled until she found out from the newspapers the news she feared so much, Siegel was murdered, and she knew that betrayals were paid with life. Virginia wanted to commit suicide and overdosed on pills, but was saved.

Luciano was sent to Sicily by the U.S. government and Virginia asked for his forgiveness. He gave her a second chance and sent her to México to expand the Mafia networks. It was 1948 and México was flourishing. Virginia went to a nightclub in México's capital and, posing as a millionaire, started talking to politicians. She was given a list of names to contact there. In México, politicians were controlled by the Mafia, including President Miguel Aleman. Tourism increased in México and casinos were set up.

Virginia was an important player at the Mafia's start in Latin America. Traveling in private planes between Sicily and México, she began to attract the attention of journalists and FBI investigations began. Virginia tried to conceal the publications in the newspapers while the FBI was preparing an offensive. The Mafia Queen fell into her own trap, she told them that she had 5 minutes left and they could send her to the United States, but the Mafia wanted to send her to Europe. The FBI got her and told them the strategy of the Mafia was facing revolutions.

THE MAFIA IN CHICAGO

- Al Capone was born in Brooklyn in 1899 and was the boss of the biggest Mafia in Chicago. He died in 1947.
- Joe Aiello, alcohol dealer and enemy of Al Capone. He was assassinated in 1930.
- Bugs Moran, an enemy of Al Capone, teamed up with Joe Aiello to kill Al Capone and take over the beer business. He died in prison in 1956.
- Frank Nitti, born in 1887, was one of the bodyguards and later, successor to Al Capone. He died by suicide in 1943.
- Sam Giancana, born in Illinois in 1908, was also a Chicago mob boss. He was assassinated in 1975.
- Joe Masseria, New York Mafia boss, was born in 1885 and murdered in 1931.
- John Scalise, a member of the Chicago gangs, was born in 1902 and shot to death in 1929.

During the Prohibition era in the United States, there were gangs of mobsters fighting for power and killing each other in the streets. Al Capone was a very dangerous man, robbing trucks, running brothels and dealing in alcohol. He had enemies from other gangs in the city and had been ambushed several times. Capone fought back and was willing to take out his enemies, especially Bugs Moran, when he orchestrated the St. Valentine's Day Massacre on February 14, 1929.

Capone's plan was to trick Moran and offer him a few cases of whiskey at a very low price, using another person to make the sale. A supposed Mr. Matute, born in Castel Gandolfo and dedicated to transportation, offered him 80 cases for cash. He asked for U$56 per case plus the operator's fee. Of the U$4,996 he asked for, he was paid only U$4,000.

He had to be there before 4pm and the trap was set to kill the boss. Don Pasquale was very proper, but they attacked each other and then had parties. «The problem with this country is that there is no order,» Al Capone rightly said. The guys smoked in the middle of the street and everyone wanted to kill him.

Everything was ready to carry out the St. Valentine's Day Massacre, Al Capone's revenge against his enemies. Early in the morning, mobsters disguised as police officers faked a raid against rival gang members. They put them against the wall, disarmed them and killed them.

Aiello, another of Chicago's gangsters, had no criminal record. He made a deal to buy a new car for U$750 that was worth U$800. He delivered it to an address, along with some machine guns. By the year 1892, Aiello had killed 30 people in 3 years. Aiello was killed by Capone a year after the St. Valentine's Day Massacre.

CHAPTER 11
KOREAN WAR

North Korea is an isolated place and the saddest place in the world, being the fourth military power. In 1950 there were many U.S. soldiers in North Korea. They fought for 3 years and Chinese, U.S. and French soldiers died. South Korea after 40 years wonders why this happened, as it looks like the third world war. They returned to Korea because of the memory of the disasters

It was a Sunday morning and nine year old Carol was attending high school. She thought it was an affair when World War II broke out. Women were used as prostitutes for the U.S. Army, who were not well received. The Soviets took over South Korea and planned to free themselves from the U.S., making the two Koreas communist. The Japanese agreed with the U.S. that the Japanese would elect the government. The idea was long overdue.

Soon in the streets strikes began, as they did not want US-Americans. A medical student began to teach the students. In 1948 they continued to protest and all did the same, preparing for war. The U.S. joined forces to invade North and South Korea, who said «we don't want war». The Chinese did not want to go to war. US-Americans thought war was far away, but it was not so unfortunately. No one told Stalin to invade South Korea and US-Americans said war will not be stopped.

On June 25, 1950 North Korea launched a war against South Korea. US-Americans condemned North Korea and Russia confronted the world. The U.S. commander said it was the fault of the imperialists.

The Chinese were unaware of the students' interventions and began to prepare themselves with medicine from the North Korean police. Forty four thousand soldiers were trapped and many surrendered. Lack of medicine turned into war.

The Communists wanted war. An 11-year-old girl returned home because her parents had been killed. As the armed Communists went to South Korea, they killed many Koreans. People did not like Koreans. South Koreans didn't resist and wanted to win the war. The door to the Americas closed.

A young man under 20 did not want to avoid clashes between Communists and separatists. A journalist told him to spy on the North Koreans and wants a confession. The journalist refuses and they are put in jail.

In September 1950 China was worried because many people were going to die. The U.S. force was thinking about how to subdue the Koreans and win a victory. It was autumn and the secret of nuclear war was looming. On November 10,

1950 the story began on the river, with a shipment of a 3-ton bomb, the largest in the United States. The pilot recruited France to drop the bomb 765 meters high and it shook the earth at a distance of 40 kilometers. The children were taken to see the disaster and an 18-year-old boy, who was not prepared for war, was astonished.

Douglas MacArthur, U.S. general, said:

«In war, you win or lose, live or die - and the difference is just an eyelash.»

The United States took revenge with its large air fleet, while people were dying from fires and suffocation. There were 200 dead in one small village.

US-Americans thought Koreans were hiding. Civilians did not join the fight; they were considered enemies. Later it was reported that they were hiding in a large village.

CHAPTER 12

U.S.-MÉXICO WAR

MEXICAN INDEPENDENCE

- In 1815 México was a colony. With the death of Morillo, the insurgency arose. They retreated to the Veracruz area where there was fishing, which they transported across a bridge. Thus began many trades.
- In 1816. Juan Luis Porlaco arrived at the court in Madrid. The men were tired of fighting for days, so the pardons of the insurgents began. The politicians of the Spanish crown, mortally wounded, preferred the pardon. The insurgent found himself in the sheep pass.
- In 1817 they decided to fight the monarch and bought swords for the insurgency. Many were shot and the insurgents' fight became difficult.

They fought with 81 men and the war was normalized. The Spaniards were tired, as the war had been going on for a long time. The insurgents were also tired and wanted to have peace and return to their businesses.

- In 1820 Rafael del Riego started a military uprising and urged King Ferdinand VII to withdraw. The Church was required and the province would increase. The King became a conspirator and for years the Crown of Spain felt contempt.

- Meanwhile, Vicente Guerrero prepared a new army in México in January 1821. He sought victory and being US-Americans, they wanted to be superior and met a loyal friend. He had political skill and thought of independence. He wanted to unite with the Catholics and did not meet reservations with the barons' families. It was a process to seek three guarantees: religion, peace and loyalty.

- In 6 months the Mexican troops occupied Guadalajara. The King of Spain complied with the rules and the Masons got in the way. The Polish King was discovered in Veracruz and the Spanish wanted to win all transfers and treaties.

- In Cordoba the liberation of México began and the last Spanish soldiers left the country. In a speech delivered by the Liberator of México, he told them: «You are free. It is up to you to get ahead.»

U.S. INTERVENTION IN MÉXICO

The United States declared war on México in 1846. In that year, the U.S. Army had crossed the Río Grande iver. The President of the United States at the time was General Polk, a charismatic and brilliant man, although he seemed over-weight to some. The U.S. Army defeated the Aztecs that same year and California fell.

For his part, Antonio López de Santa Anna returned from asylum and made a speech dedicated to México, which allowed him to return. He was the only one capable of over-throwing the United States. In 1847, Santa Anna organized the army with 20,000 men, of which 15,000 survived. The Mexican guerrilla committed atrocities with the military and sometimes it was thought that they were helping the U.S.s.

The U.S. Army, under the command of General Scott, advanced through the areas of Saltillo and Veracruz. Scott was hated by all, due to his appearance. The army commanded by Santa Anna went hungry and cold, with many dead and dying, but he wanted to move forward.

During one of the most important battles, the Battle of Angostura, Mexican and U.S. troops met on a rainy and windy night. General Manuel María Lombardini attacked the U.S. troops from the front, who attacked them with artillery batteries. Many U.S. soldiers died, but the Mexicans fared worse. Santa Anna did not think they would fare so badly and seeing that there was no victory, he relied on the Catholic Church, which helped him with expenses.

Santa Anna was on the verge of being overthrown after this battle. Ten thousand U.S. soldiers were waiting for him in Veracruz and he resigned himself to his fate. On the other hand, General Scott had arrived in Veracruz and the battles and bombardments continued. There was no end to the wounded and dead on both sides and it was estimated that more than 6,000 U.S. guns were fired. Santa Anna said: «Every nation has its destiny. It is not in the hands of the U.S., it is in our hands.»

On April 14, Scott had 6,500 men and Santa Anna had 14,500. During the night, Scott settled in the hills and before 10 a.m. the battle was over, with much loss to the Mexicans. From General Scott's point of view, he had lost to Santa Anna and was looking at how to rebuild the army as the war dragged on. His army thought it was the people's soldiers. Santa Anna believed that the U.S. would not be able to move supplies and could surround him. For his part, Scott thought this battle was a poor man's mission lost.

At that time, a writer from the U.S. wrote that these two nations should have no ceasefire. Between the summit of two volcanoes the small army of 4,000 men hid with much trouble. The Spaniards had built a church on the summit. Scott wanted to move on, but the U.S. soldiers were disoriented. Another general thought the Mexicans could not defeat them.

In 1847, General Scott thought he could win by crossing the mountain, so he reversed course. He was two days from the city of Puebla. He was following the same path as Cortez, who 300 years earlier had been unable to do anything. Scott traveled over the mountain and left the army in that city, saying that «that city will be ours.» Another U.S. general thought they could not win, for the city was too big. The bells were ringing.

General Santa Anna rebuilt the army and arrived with 25,000 men, who marched against the U.S. army with old weapons, but Scott was lucky. During the Battle of Padierna, the more ambitious General Gabriel Valencia planned to win. They saw 23,000 U.S. soldiers crossing and Scott thought it was going well. Valencia's idea of retreat was to cross the river, but Santa Anna found the crossing difficult. After 3 days Scott's forces lost 10,000 U.S. soldiers.

Despite losing several battles, Santa Anna wanted to remain in command at full force. José Fernández Ramírez wanted to see what was going on and said: «tell my family that we have lost. Our souls are broken.» Nicola wanted a peace agreement, but none of Santa Anna's generals wanted to accept. He suspended failed negotiations.

Scott planned to restructure the army, but it was not to be. At the Battle of King's Mill he thought he would find powder and ammunition, but there was none. The battle lasted two hours. Scott lost, but Santa Anna had more losses. The bells were ringing, nothing could be done.

The Mexican army wanted to see where U.S. troops could enter during the Battle of Chapultepec. The battle lasted 14 hours and they did not lose. Santa Anna wanted more men for his army, but no one was sent. Colonel Juan Cano asked an uncle: «Tell my brother not to come to Chapultepec. I don't want my poor father to be left without children».

Four hundred snipers climbed the hill and even the cadets fought, including a 13 year old boy who had fallen dead. The U.S.s knocked down Chapultepec Castle and the

Mexicans surrendered, for they had failed. In the early morning of September 14, General Scott had gone up to throw stones at the enemy army.

After losing the battles, Santa Anna returned to the asylum and distanced himself from the majority. «I never did anything wrong against my country», he said. Santa Anna, once rich, lost everything and the only thing he had left was his wife.

Nicholas Trist, a U.S. diplomat sent to México during the war, had never been on a mission. He was suspended by the U.S. soldiers for disobeying orders during negotiations to end the war. He had never fought. A Mexican wrote to Trist and he disobeyed his superiors, writing a 46-page document.

As compensation for México losing the war, the U.S.s wanted to give them U$15,000,000, but they did not accept it. If México accepted the sale, they would receive U.S. citizenship, but they did not accept. On February 19, 1848 they signed the peace agreement.

Many Mexicans opposed becoming U.S. citizens. They said «we are defeated and many have died. Our people have the right to live in peace. We lost California and La Mesa and we are receiving U$15,000,000. We accept defeat.

On May 30, peace was finally established and they had a life ahead of them. The Mexicans have never forgotten this, as it is a mutilation of their territory. The veteran Mexican fighters paraded proudly after their defeat.

Guillermo Duque said: «In México we lost territory but we have the experience of organizing our nation ourselves. It is difficult to assimilate this great defeat. The U.S. won».

In 1865 the U.S. clenched their hands, celebrating such an infamous action against such a small nation. The land they expropriated in California was rich, having gold and minerals. None of the Mexicans accepted U.S. citizenship. Mariano Vallejo was a very important character in the transition of California from Mexican to U.S. territory. They started a garden with his land and when he died in 1896, he left one hectare of land, some cows and the experience of not fighting.

Thomas Nelson Jr. said that the fight came to nothing. Today the war is a very important case study but the experience lived by the two countries is obligatory to live it together.

CHAPTER 13
LEONARDO DA VINCI

Leonardo Da Vinci was the son of a slave named Caterina. The history of Mediterranean slavery is found in Venezia. He was a great painter of much fame and was one of the best painters in the world.

CHAPTER 14
INVENTOR OF LIGHT

Marconi dreamed 1000 nights and could not complete the dream that created the lights. One day he looked at two stones and made them shine. He thought that with this he could have light and began to study. Little by little he invented lights.

CHAPTER 15

CRISTOFORO COLOMBO

C ristoforo Colombo, known in Castilian as Cristóbal Colón and in English as Christopher Columbus, was a Genoese sailor. He had a dream that beyond the sea there was life and asked the Italian government for help, but they had no way to help him. He went to Queen Isabella in Spain and she gave him three ships: the Niña, the Pinta and the Santa María. She also gave him men that she took out of the prisons who were very dangerous prisoners.

They traveled night and day without rest, until his crew got fed up and wanted to kill him and throw him into the sea. Finally someone said that there was land and so America was discovered. They saw that there were people living in what is now the United States and other parts of the continent.

CHAPTER 16

THE MIRACLE OF JOSÉ GREGORIO HERNÁNDEZ

I am Teresa Di Sclafani and in 1967 I received a miracle. My son Vincenzo had a fever. At three o'clock in the afternoon I gave him a remedy and his fever went down at seven o'clock, then he fell asleep at eight o'clock. When I went to look at him he was shaking. I gave him his medicine and his fever did not go down, so I gave him a suppository. At midnight he died, he stopped breathing. I summoned Doctor José Gregorio Hernández with all my strength and after half an hour he started to breathe.

We went to the Calicanto clinic and he had a fever of 43 degrees Celsius (109.4 Fahrenheit). They put him in a bathtub with water and ice and the fever diminished. The next day he had sores in his mouth.

In gratitude I took a plaque to José Gregorio Hernández to Trujillo, where he was born, and one to Caracas, where he is buried. He performed many miracles but the Pope did not recognize them because the sorcerers work with his spirit.

On April 30, 2021, a girl had an accident, which caused a tumor in her head and then disappeared. This miracle was recognized by the Pope and José Gregorio was beatified.

With this in mind, I decided to have a statue made in Palermo Italy, the town where my husband, Alia, was born. I called Father Antonino Vicari and he told me that he did not know this blessing. He called the Vatican and was told that he was blessed, so I started the procedures with Bishop Giuseppe Marchante.

It took me three months to get the authorization to place it in a small church at the entrance of the town of Santa Rosalia. The statue was made by the best sculptor in the world, who works for the Vatican. The statue is 170 centimeters high and 10 centimeters at the base.

Living in Florida I could not do it directly and I called my niece Santina's husband, Giuseppe Nogara, who is a military man and is very Catholic. He made all the arrangements and I went to Italy on June 18 when they performed the blessings. Monsignor Di Sclafani, Father Mormino, the author, Father Antonino Vicari, parish priest of Mother Church and Santa Anna. Also in attendance were the clergy, the sisterhood of the Mother of Grace San Giuseppe and Divine Providence, musicians and the whole town.

My nephew spoke about the life of the Blessed José Gregorio Hernández and then I spoke, giving testimony of the miracle. The Di Sclafani family made history.

CHAPTER 17
POPE FRANCIS

Pope Francis on September 12, 2023, criticized the Ukrainian right wing and said he agreed with Russia. He said that mighty Russia was against the Republic.

The Pope admired Perón's policies. At that time children were kidnapped, a nun and a priest and sold to blacks, but the Pope never said anything. After many years they returned to their homes with grown children and their wives. Some mothers are alive and some are dead. Everyday women go to walk to the Plaza de Mayo to claim their children and this is their sad story.

CHAPTER 18

FRANCISCO DE MIRANDA

Francisco de Miranda was born in Caracas in 1750. His father was an islander and married his mother while she was pregnant. His mother had 9 surviving children and several stillbirths, Miranda being the eldest of them all. At the time of his birth, the population of Venezuela was made up of whites, blacks, Indians and mestizos.

In childhood he had the best teachers and was very intelligent. He studied at military school and reached the rank of General. Despite being close to many beautiful society women, he never married. He spoke English, Italian and Castilian.

He had problems with England, Spain and France for his pro-independence ideas. He fought against the Spanish to liberate the important island of Cuba and against the French to liberate the great city of New Orleans, near the Mississippi

River. He was imprisoned several times, but nothing was ever proven against him.

He lived for a time in France, from where they wanted to expel him. He argued that they could not, since he paid taxes. Miranda arrived in Holland and was presented to the Minister of France, who referred him to the Prefect. He then went to the minister of police, who presented him to the consul and explained to them why he returned to France. He said that he did not want to confront anyone, he only wanted resources to survive, because the Republic was his patrimony.

She was given a passport stating that Miranda was 46 years old and 1.78 meters tall. He should be allowed to go to Paris without any problems. As soon as he was given the passport, the consul, a friend of Miranda's, took measures to make him leave and found away. Napoleon agreed with Miranda's presence and he could live in Paris or in any part of France, under peculiar conditions until he was free.

Napoleon arrived in Paris on August 30, 1800 and the next day he told his minister Joseph Fouché to arrange every-thing and left for the United States. Miranda visited his friend Marquise De Custine, who was at that time in love with Fouché. She interceded on Miranda's behalf to continue with personal influence, as it was a political case. A few days later, the police showed up at Miranda's house, accusing him of conspiring against France, when in fact Miranda was conspiring against Spain, which was a friend of France.

She was given another passport stating that she was 47 years old and 1.76 meters tall. On March 17, 1801, she left France for England and soon became Chateaubriand's fervent love. Miranda, that game that Napoleon had, for not pushing to get ahead.

On May 13, a few months after his arrival, the new ministers received him with friendship and with civil and military plans, all in secret. England gave him political, military and financial support. These were the documents that accused him, drawn up in France and Spain. The Spanish crown wanted the sovereignty of America, neither by papal donations nor by the right of conquest. Spain sent a deputy to the congress.

Miranda sought independence and freedom for several countries in the Americas, with the following ideals:

- The Catholic religion would be the main religion, but other religions would be tolerated.
- Ecclesiastical functions were declared incompatible with civil functions.
- Indigenous people of color would enjoy the rights of citizenship.
- Every citizen from 18 to 58 years of age was obliged to take up arms in defense of the homeland.
- The slaves were excluded. Miranda drew a lot of distance and seemed to forget them.
- Prisoners of war were to be cared for generously and with dignity.
- Mistreatment of civilians with military columns was prohibited.
- Illicit trade, unregulated peddlers and prostitution were subject to imprisonment.

- Miranda set very correct standards in Panama, complying with U.S. government wishes. He presented projects in Curaçao and designed the flag of Venezuela in yellow, blue and red.

HE PLANNED that the landing would be in Coro, Venezuela, where the inhabitants were in favor of independence and without defense. A corps of 2000 men and 300 horses was formed to continue to San Felipe, Nirgua and Valencia. He planned to use the Roman system and left forts to hold the center line from Curaçao to Valencia. He also wanted to seek reinforcements and make a movement to the Aragua Valley through Maracay, San Mateo and La Victoria, an area heavily populated by people prone to independence. A maritime force leaving from Grenada and Trinidad would attack Cumaná and La Guaira. In this way, Caracas would be taken between two forces and thus the forces of the province would be reduced and success would be assured.

Trinidad could be penetrated through the Orinoco. Once Caracas was controlled, an important armed force would leave for Maracaibo, Riohacha, Santa Marta and Cartagena, cutting off the Magdalena exit. The communications of New Grenada would be closed. To prevent relief being sent from Havana to Cartagena, the British school would blockade the port against the Isthmus of Panama, and then send a maritime force through Panama to the southern seas of Peru and Chile. Once Panama was controlled, the next aim was the Caribbean and the Gulf of México near Jamaica, Cuba and Florida.

The rest of the continent was unknown. From Trinidad a maritime attack would be launched through La Guaira and Cumaná, while by land it transit through Coro. Miranda did not believe in it. He could go by Bogotá from Trinidad and Angostura, which crossed two rivers, integrated by plains and mountains with very difficult natural obstacles from Maracaibo and Cartagena. The Atlantic coast of Panama was not so useful to pass through to the Pacific, much less to control Chile and Peru.

Napoleon and President Adams were right, seeing in Miranda a Don Quixote, a dreamer who struggled with the impossible. The English officers thought differently from Miranda and what Miranda longed for was the freedom of America.

The British fleet led by Nelson in the fortress of Denmark, on April 2, 1801, ended those coalitions of the English against Switzerland. In the Mediterranean the British achieved another success: the battle of Alexandria. The movements continued in France by the Treaty of Aranjuez, which on March 21, 1801 ceded Louisiana to Spain and left the right to recover it with the Treaty of Badajoz. In 1801 Portuguese ports were closed to England and Portugal ceded part of Guyana to France.

Bonaparte achieved the peace of Rome on July 15, 1801. Everyone thought of England's peace with France and its preparations, without suspending a possible invasion. France abandoned its pretensions in Egypt and England and would keep Tobago, Martinique, the Essequibo and Trinidad. There was strong debate in the English parliament and it was dissolved with general elections. Russia and Austria would not confront Napoleon and he wanted to use Santo Domingo as a colonial base to receive the new Louisiana.

In a maneuver on May 2, 1803, France sold the territory to the United States. The English atmosphere was untenable. Addington resigned on April 29, 1804 and was replaced on May 12 of the same year. That change deepened the Emperor's proclamation. The Duke of Enghien had just been executed by General Hulin, on suspicion of treason against Bonaparte.

There was a concern that the French troops would reach the British Isles through the channel, which forced the English government to carry out a military operation. In view of this, Mr. Robert R Livingston, chancellor and minister of the United States in Paris and known to Miranda, went to London to propose to Napoleon to manipulate Austria and Russia. Napoleon controlled Charles IV, who controlled all of Italy. He accused as a unique case Tsar Alexander I, who refused to submit to the emperor.

Addington during his ministry had approved of the Spanish revolutions and preferred freedom to run Spain. He neglected English interests in retaliation from Spain and France.

On October 4, 1804 the English attacked four Spanish ships loaded with Peruvian treasure. In view of this fact, on December 12, 1804, Spain was forced to declare war with England. Before the war between England and Spain and after seizing the Spanish ships, there was a meeting between

Pitt and Sir Henry Dundas (Lord Melville) that dealt with South America. Captain Admiral Sir Home Popham was commissioned, who met with Miranda and saw the intentions of the British regarding America.

Miranda reconsidered his military plans due to Popham's influence to introduce notable changes when he learned of Miranda's ideas and the British project. He changed his planned entry point by the Caribbean coast and Cartagena, ceased land and sea operations on Caracas, which he changed to a strong attack on Trinidad and Barbados. Once Caracas and Santa Fe de Bogotá were dominated, he could prepare other expeditions, always with citizens' support. He planned attacks on Santa Marta from Maracaibo, with missions leaving from Jamaica and also an attack on the Gulf of Darien, to take the position of Panama with respect to the Pacific.

It was consistent with the idea of Panama as a base, with 4000 men by ship coming from India to embark for Lima and Valparaiso. Another force of 3000 men was to attack Buenos Aires, for U.S. effect and the fight on the Pacific side with the Atlantic coast.

Spain was becoming more and more dependent on France and dangerous for England. The manufacturing exports were the main support of Spain. To receive U.S. wealth, it was surviving through the maritime traffic of U.S. merchandise. Popham considered that the independence of America meant destruction of Spanish wealth, with potential reduction of its fleet and avoidance of a strengthened French fleet.

In the face of a possible war with England, the independence of Spanish America was of great interest to England, unique in its existence. Whatever the plans of the diplomat Miranda, he wanted to go to Trinidad in a private capacity to create disharmony with Jovian, served the treasury, the navy and the local government with the interactions of Henry Dundas, already Viscount de Melville.

Miranda considered a new project to go forward from London. Dundas, a friend of Pitt, was a minister between 1794 and 1801 as secretary of war. Miranda made an analysis which he presented to the Viscount with certain elements for immediate action. Mr. Vansittart's warning about the opinions of the English government, who said the time had not come to act with such possibilities. The United States Minister to the English court, Mr. Rufus King, on his return trip from the United States conceded that the English government refused to approve the actions.

On his way to the United States, Miranda explained that Washington, Knox and Hamilton had promised assistance to help the troops, while the English government refused or was unable to help them. Miranda wanted to impress them and persuade England to use its navy as support. We have mentioned that Nicholas Vansittart, future Baron del Rey, was not only a friend of Miranda, but also his direct contact with the English government. Vansittart was Minister and Secretary to the Treasury until May 1804 and a few months later, in January 1805, Mr. Pitt joined the Ministry as Secretary for Ireland.

At the end of 1804 and half of 1805, Miranda went to London carrying on certain conversations with Lord Melville, Home Popham, Sir Evan Nepean, John Tumbull and others, under the eye of Prime Minister Pitt. He made invitations, reports and calculations, while the European course changed. Admiral Nelson defeated the Spanish and French fleets at the Battle of Trafalgar on October 21, 1805, giving England control of the sea.

Then Napoleon was triumphant atAusterlitz on December 2, 1805 against the Russians and Austrians and gained domination of continental Europe. It was inevitable that England and Napoleon would confront each other and one would dominate the other. Under such the English policies were oriented.

Another important consideration and interest was the exact dimensions of England vis-à-vis Miranda, the statements of Lord Melville and his consultations. A new alliance against France replaced the U.S. issue with a more urgent one. Miranda suspended travel to Trinidad at the moment of departure under frivolous pretexts, of an annoying decision. The imbecility reached its peak, the interests of our country could not be eliminated. In spite of the tragic death of Alexander Hamilton, he was to move to the United States.

Miranda felt insulted by the guarantee that Mr. Pitt made him request, barely installed in the government. If Miranda left England, he could do nothing in Trinidad without the Governor's consent. It was Pitt's belief that a favorable course from England could not attack Spaniards but if the opposite happened, any inconvenience Spain might suffer would be good for England.

The U.S. representative in London in 1798, Mr. Rufus King, had recognized the situation and informed his government. England, since Miranda's arrival here and without his knowledge, informed Spain that it would not give any assistance to the Spanish colonies for their independence. He joined forces with the Spanish in order to reject the French teachings and pressures against Spanish and Portuguese rule. The Kings were briefed by Miranda for an expedition to Trinidad that suspended collaborations with the United States.

Miranda, impatient for the success of the enterprises and ignorant of the Englishman's decision, sent a commissioner to the United States, with Sir Evan Nepean and Vansittart making changes. Finally, Sir Pitt, through the aforementioned gentlemen, made Miranda aware of his aspirations about his integrity and honesty.

Plans were unfeasible during the month of July 1805 in view of the last negotiations with Prime Minister Pitt, who advised Miranda to wait a little. «For political business in Europe we have to start another cargo company». Miranda, overruled, would not take the blame and it was not possible for Pitt to inform Miranda of the attacks to be executed by England, because of the naval maneuvers against him with France and Spain.

Miranda and the English government reached an agreement, in which Miranda accepted England's decision. It was seen with U.S. interest to support Miranda and all his powers. Miranda would send people in England secret correspondence. With English authority, he would give an account of his English Squadron that was in the area where he was to be involved.

It was when Miranda realized that Mr. Pitt had been negotiating for a long time through negotiations, to include:

- England's commitment not to disturb the Spanish colonies or allow the use of its possessions for revolutionary work on the continent.

- Spain's commitment not to attack Portugal and to maintain its integrity and independence.

To communicate privately with Miranda, he had to leave England and go to the United States. Vansittart provided him with a document of inestimable political and diplomatic value. It was a letter to King, dated London, August 14, 1805, which explained the English position regarding Miranda and his projects. Vansittart mentioned that his letters were sent through a friend.

Miranda embarked on his great plan for the liberation of his country. Miranda went alone, without support or help. For Miranda, this document was of great political and diplomatic value. Vansittart was again, in January 1805, a member of the cabinet and therefore thought that the document had been drafted, signed and delivered with Pitt's consent.

Mr. Vansittart knew that note would be in King's hands. It had to be with the U.S. government, which is why the tone of the letter's contents were of special subtlety. The English political game was very clear in international situations. It was not possible for England to immediately support Miranda's projects against Spain. They were interested in free trade with Spanish America, an activity that had been denied by Spain. Mr. King knew it and England was sure that it would achieve that objective.

An independent and secure government was being installed. Faced with this prospect, the English politicians were ready with the word freedom and were very well aware of the international situations. Vansittart was sure that Miranda would have important success with favorable English public opinion. To prevent Spain or France from giving reinforcements to America to stop Miranda's revolutionary actions, the English government ordered its war troops to be vigilant.

«I address you with the confidence of a friend, with British feeling for the interests of the country of England.» Miranda's influence met his last will and several dangerous political risks. He worked much of his life for this moment. His first son, whom he named Leandro, was 18 months old. Becoming a father for the first time at age 55 was a moment to remember.

With his few goods, his archives and his library, Miranda used his will to summarize his own life that he considered consecrated for political plans, to ensure that Hispanics had wise civil liberties. With that good intention he fought for his compatriots. He wrote an emotional testament for the attainment of freedom for the homeland, the people and the destiny of its citizens. Taught by the University of Caracas, it is a special letter because of its basis.

Miranda was in debt to three booksellers, Messrs. Dulati, White and Evan had given him several books, which he had to return if he did not pay for them. He wrote to three friends: Rufus King, William & Smith of New York and Christopher Gore of Boston. He advised them of his early arrival and asked King and Gore to meet to discuss important matters. He wanted them to be ready to act and asked Smith to be ready to do business. He considered himself the victor.

On 2 September 1805 Miranda embarked on the ship Polly at Gravesend. On November 9 he arrived in New York and communicated with Mr. King. He sent him Vansittart's letters and soon launched a military expedition. He lacked abundant funds and had to find out how to act in the territory of the United States.

The status of the United States that Miranda discovered after his travels in 1783 and 1785, was that three states had been added: Kentucky in 1792, Tennessee in 1796 and Ohio in 1803. The U.S. is led for the second time by Mr. John Adams, successor to Washington, founder of the Republic, member of Congress. He participated in the Act of Independence, acted as governor of Virginia, minister to the United States and France, vice-president of the United States in France and vice-president of the United States in 1797 and 1801.

Elected in 1804, Jefferson's presence in the White House was very significant. It had not happened before in the politiics of the republican federalist country. It changed presidential life, the relations of the President and his secretaries, with Congress and with the U.S. people. Latin and Greek history was studied to avoid tyranny.

During Jefferson's first term, the United States purchased Louisiana from France for U$10,000,000. In addition to this immense territory to the country, the U.S. government settled its relations with France.

Miranda's plans had repercussions in the Democratic-ordered government, culminating in the U.S. Congressional court in New York. Miranda had to take care of the financing of his expeditions for U.S. interests. Upon arrival in New York, he gave Mr. King the letters of Vansittart, considering it very important to think of Great Britain with respect to Spanish America. For this reason nothing could be done by the government at that time, in connection with the achievement pursued by General Miranda. He dealt with the U.S. authority and, making good use of King's notes to Madison, he moved to Washington.

He left New York on November 29 and kept a diary, as he usually did. He noted on that visit a letter to President John Adams, where he was informed about commerce, agriculture and construction.

On April 5, 1815, Dr. Benjamin Busch was informed that General Miranda had visited Philadelphia and went to dinner with him, where he discussed political relations and the court of Europe. The day after arriving in Washington, Miranda visited the President. He was aware of King's note to Vansittart's letter and carried an immediate letter of introduction.

Dispatching his ministers, he asked him how he left Europe, since apparently they were all armed. Miranda took leave to go to the Secretary of State also. Doctor Busch spoke with Mr. Madison, who received him with pleasure, saying that he had several U.S. political items to communicate to the President.

Without wasting time, on Monday the 9th Madison summoned Miranda to his office for Tuesday the 10th at 2 PM, but Miranda was absent. The appointment was not kept until Thursday the 12th. They were very private conversations, according to the President's instructions. Miranda said he had told Secretary Madison that he had made every effort to emancipate the Spanish American continent, but the consent of the government was needed. He had friends in New York and Boston who offered them funds and that the government would lend them assistance and approve the note that England was providing for some part of the continent. The Secretary heard the proposal with pleasure, but they were concerned about England, which in possession of some part of another continent could help the government.

Upon arriving at his hotel, Miranda found a card from President Jefferson, inviting him to dinner on the 13th. The day before dinner Miranda's interview with the Secretary of State continued. It was a very peculiar conversation that did not respond to any particular enterprise. He manifested that the government had the best will towards Miranda. The way of acting was more adventurous and dangerous than to help it properly by the government.

Miranda was a world fighter, uniting countries. He was imprisoned several times and died alone. Nobody remembered the good he did all over the world. He needed 50 pounds and 300 pesos for himself. They were delivered but it was necessary to spend the money. The plan was not fulfilled nor was any other bribe.

By the end of March 1816, the pressure on him was too much. Seriously ill, in pain, disillusioned, sad and helpless, no one remembered him. The help offered never arrived. On the 25th of that month he suffered a stroke and lasted several weeks in very bad shape. On July 14, 1816, at five minutes past one in the morning, he gave up his spirit, as his servant Moran wrote to Mr. Peter Turnbull.

About the Author

Teresa Di Sclafani De Nasca was born in Italy. She has also lived in Venezuela and in the United States. Her autobiography will be published soon.

www.ingramcontent.com/pod-product-compliance
Lightning Source LLC
Chambersburg PA
CBHW020333130626
46549CB00003B/1156